Table Of Contents

Chapter 1: Understanding AI and DeepSeek

What is Artificial Intelligence?

Artificial Intelligence (AI) refers to the simulation of human intelligence processes by machines, particularly computer systems. This technology encompasses various capabilities, including learning, reasoning, problem-solving, perception, and language understanding. AI systems are designed to analyze data and make decisions based on the information they process. As a user, understanding the foundational concepts of AI is essential for effectively leveraging tools like DeepSeek, which harness this technology to enhance productivity and creativity.

At the core of AI is machine learning, a subset that enables systems to improve their performance over time without being explicitly programmed. Machine learning algorithms analyze patterns in data and learn from them, allowing the system to make predictions or decisions based on new inputs. Deep learning, a further advancement in machine learning, uses neural networks with many layers to analyze complex data sets, such as images or natural language. Understanding these concepts is crucial for users who wish to navigate the functionalities of DeepSeek successfully.

AI can be categorized into two main types: narrow AI and general AI. Narrow AI refers to systems designed to perform specific tasks, such as virtual assistants, recommendation systems, or image recognition tools. These applications are prevalent in everyday life and are the primary focus of most current AI developments. General AI, on the other hand, represents a theoretical concept where machines possess the ability to understand, learn, and apply intelligence across a wide range of tasks, similar to human capabilities. While general AI remains largely aspirational, narrow AI is already transforming various industries, including finance, healthcare, and entertainment.

The impact of AI on society is profound, influencing how individuals interact with technology and each other. AI-powered tools can automate mundane tasks, analyze vast amounts of data quickly, and provide insights that were previously unattainable. Users of technologies like DeepSeek can harness these capabilities to enhance their work processes, make better decisions, and unlock new levels of creativity. As AI continues to evolve, its integration into daily life will become increasingly seamless, further demonstrating its potential to augment human capabilities.

Understanding artificial intelligence is essential for users looking to master tools such as DeepSeek. By grasping the basic principles of AI, its types, and its societal implications, users can effectively utilize DeepSeek to tap into AI's vast potential. As AI technology advances, staying informed about its developments will empower users to adapt and thrive in an increasingly digital landscape, ensuring they can harness the benefits of AI to achieve their personal and professional goals.

Introduction to DeepSeek

DeepSeek is revolutionizing the way users interact with artificial intelligence. This innovative tool harnesses the power of deep learning algorithms to analyze vast amounts of data, uncovering patterns and insights that were previously difficult to access. Designed for users at all skill levels, DeepSeek simplifies the complexities of AI, enabling individuals to leverage its capabilities without needing extensive technical knowledge. As businesses and individuals seek to optimize their decision-making processes, DeepSeek stands out as a powerful ally in the quest for data-driven solutions.

At its core, DeepSeek operates by utilizing advanced neural networks to process information. These networks mimic the human brain's functioning, allowing the tool to learn from data inputs and improve its accuracy over time. Users can input various types of data, including text, images, and numerical values, and DeepSeek will analyze this information to provide meaningful insights. This capability makes DeepSeek not only versatile but also an invaluable resource for tackling a wide range of challenges, from market analysis to predictive modeling.

One of the key features that sets DeepSeek apart is its user-friendly interface. Designed with the end-user in mind, the platform allows users to navigate its functionalities with ease, minimizing the learning curve typically associated with AI tools. The intuitive dashboard provides access to various analytical functions and visualizations, making it straightforward for users to interpret the results of their queries. As a result, individuals can focus more on deriving insights rather than getting bogged down by technical complexities.

DeepSeek is also equipped with a robust set of functionalities that cater to different user needs. Whether one is interested in conducting sentiment analysis on social media data, forecasting sales trends, or identifying customer segments, DeepSeek offers tailored solutions. This adaptability ensures that users can apply the tool across various domains and industries, enhancing its utility and relevance. By addressing specific use cases, DeepSeek empowers users to tackle their unique challenges effectively.

As we delve deeper into the capabilities of DeepSeek, it becomes evident that this tool is not merely a trend but a transformative technology that can unlock the full potential of AI for users. By bridging the gap between complex AI methodologies and practical application, DeepSeek invites everyone to explore the possibilities of data-driven insights. Understanding its foundational concepts will pave the way for users to master this powerful tool and harness its advantages in their personal and professional endeavors.

The Importance of AI in Today's World

Artificial Intelligence (AI) has become an integral part of modern society, influencing various aspects of daily life and industry. Its importance lies in its ability to enhance efficiency, drive innovation, and solve complex problems. In today's fast-paced world, organizations are increasingly relying on AI technologies to process vast amounts of data, automate routine tasks, and improve decision-making. This reliance on AI not only streamlines operations but also leads to significant cost savings and improved productivity, making it a critical component for businesses looking to remain competitive.

One of the key areas where AI is making a profound impact is in data analysis. Traditional methods of data processing can be time-consuming and often fail to reveal deeper insights hidden within large datasets. AI, particularly through tools like DeepSeek, allows users to harness advanced algorithms that can analyze and interpret data at unprecedented speeds. This capability empowers organizations to gain actionable insights quickly, enabling them to make informed decisions based on real-time information. As data continues to grow exponentially, the importance of AI in managing and deriving value from this data cannot be overstated.

Furthermore, AI is revolutionizing customer experience across various industries. With the ability to analyze customer behavior and preferences, AI-driven tools can provide personalized recommendations and support. This level of customization leads to increased customer satisfaction and loyalty, which are essential for business growth. For instance, businesses leveraging AI can identify trends and predict future customer needs, ensuring that they stay ahead of the competition. As users of AI tools like DeepSeek begin to master these capabilities, they can significantly enhance their engagement with customers, thereby driving revenue and strengthening brand loyalty.

In addition to improving operational efficiency and customer relations, AI plays a vital role in innovation. By automating routine tasks and providing deep insights, AI frees up valuable time for employees to focus on creative problem-solving and strategic initiatives. This shift not only fosters a more innovative workplace culture but also encourages collaboration among teams. As users become proficient in utilizing AI tools, they can experiment with new ideas and solutions, leading to breakthroughs that can redefine industries and improve overall quality of life.

Lastly, the ethical implications of AI cannot be ignored. As AI systems become more prevalent, it is essential for users to understand the ethical considerations surrounding their use. Issues such as data privacy, security, and algorithmic bias are critical topics that need to be addressed. By fostering a responsible approach to AI deployment, users can ensure that technology serves the greater good, promoting fairness and accountability. As the importance of

5

AI continues to evolve, embracing these ethical principles will be essential for creating a sustainable future where AI benefits all members of society.

Chapter 2: Getting Started with DeepSeek

Installing DeepSeek

Installing DeepSeek requires a systematic approach to ensure a smooth setup process. First, you need to check the system requirements for DeepSeek to verify that your computer meets the necessary specifications. Typically, these specifications include a compatible operating system, sufficient RAM, and adequate disk space. Familiarizing yourself with the requirements will help prevent any potential issues during installation. It is advisable to have at least 8 GB of RAM and a modern multi-core processor to run DeepSeek efficiently.

Once you have confirmed that your system meets the requirements, the next step is to download the installation package. Visit the official DeepSeek website or a verified distribution platform to obtain the latest version of the software. Ensure that you are downloading from a trusted source to avoid any security risks. After the download is complete, locate the installation file in your downloads folder and proceed to run it. Depending on your operating system, you may need to grant permission for the installation process to begin.

During the installation process, you will be prompted to choose the installation directory. By default, DeepSeek will suggest a location on your primary drive, but you can change this if preferred. It is recommended to keep the default settings unless you have specific reasons to alter them, as this can help with the software's functionality and updates in the future. Follow the on-screen instructions carefully, and you may be asked to agree to the software's terms and conditions before proceeding.

After the installation is complete, you will need to configure DeepSeek to suit your preferences. Launch the application for the first time, and you will be guided through an initial setup wizard. This wizard will help you customize settings such as language preferences, database connections, and user interface options. Taking the time to adjust these settings according to your needs can enhance your overall experience with the tool and allow for better integration into your workflow.

Finally, it is essential to check for updates after installing DeepSeek. Software developers frequently release updates to improve performance, add features, and address security vulnerabilities. By navigating to the update section within the application, you can ensure that you are using the most current version of DeepSeek. Regularly checking for updates will keep your software running smoothly and help you take full advantage of its capabilities as you begin to explore the powerful functionalities DeepSeek offers.

Setting Up Your Environment

Creating an optimal environment for utilizing DeepSeek is crucial for maximizing its potential. The first step involves ensuring that your hardware meets the necessary specifications. DeepSeek, being an AI-driven tool, requires a robust processor, ample RAM, and a compatible graphics card. A minimum of 16GB of RAM is recommended for smooth operation, especially when working with larger datasets. Additionally, having a dedicated GPU can significantly enhance the processing speed for tasks such as data analysis and model training. Before proceeding, check your system's specifications against the requirements listed on the DeepSeek website to ensure compatibility.

Once your hardware is set up, the next step is to install the necessary software. DeepSeek is compatible with various operating systems, including Windows, macOS, and Linux. Depending on your system, download the appropriate version of DeepSeek from the official website. It is also advised to have Python installed, as many AI tasks within DeepSeek leverage Python libraries. Using a package manager like Anaconda can simplify the installation of Python and its associated libraries, ensuring that you have the latest versions of essential packages like NumPy, Pandas, and TensorFlow.

Configuration of the DeepSeek environment is another critical aspect. After installation, initiate the setup process by configuring the application settings to suit your workflow. This includes setting up your preferred user interface, adjusting performance settings, and customizing the toolbars to access frequently used features more efficiently. Additionally, consider creating project folders and establishing a clear directory structure to organize your datasets, models, and outputs. A well-structured project environment will facilitate easier navigation and management of your work as you delve deeper into using DeepSeek.

Networking capabilities also play a significant role in enhancing your experience with DeepSeek. For collaborative projects or research, setting up a version control system like Git can be beneficial. This allows multiple users to work on the same project while keeping track of changes made to the code and datasets. Furthermore, consider connecting with online forums or communities dedicated to DeepSeek users. Engaging with others can provide valuable insights, troubleshooting tips, and shared resources that can enrich your learning experience.

Finally, familiarize yourself with DeepSeek's documentation and tutorials. The official documentation offers a wealth of knowledge, including walkthroughs for various features and functionalities. Taking the time to explore these resources will help you understand the tool's capabilities and how to leverage them effectively. Additionally, participating in online courses or webinars can further enhance your understanding. With the right environment set up, you will be well-equipped to embark on your journey of mastering DeepSeek and unlocking its powerful AI potential.

Navigating the User Interface

Navigating the user interface of DeepSeek is essential for users to effectively harness the power of this AI tool. Upon logging into the platform, users are greeted with a clean and intuitive dashboard that serves as the command center for all activities. The design prioritizes ease of use, ensuring that even those unfamiliar with advanced technology can quickly acclimate to the environment. Key components of the interface include the main navigation bar, which provides access to different functionalities, and the workspace area, where users can interact with the AI and manage their projects.

The main navigation bar is strategically positioned at the top of the screen, featuring icons and labels that direct users to crucial sections such as 'Projects,' 'Data Management,' 'Analysis Tools,' and 'Settings.' Each section is designed with clear headings and subheadings that guide users without overwhelming them. For instance, within the 'Projects' section, users can create new projects, view existing ones, and access templates that can simplify the setup process. The layout is designed to minimize clicks and streamline workflows, making it easier for users to focus on their tasks rather than getting lost in a sea of options.

In the workspace area, users will find the tools they need to interact with the AI effectively. This area is customizable, allowing users to arrange their tools according to their preferences. On the left side, a panel displays available tools such as data upload options, analysis models, and visualization features. Users can drag and drop these tools into their workspace, facilitating a hands-on approach to managing their AI tasks. This flexibility not only enhances user experience but also encourages experimentation, as users can easily rearrange tools to discover new workflows and solutions.

Understanding the importance of real-time feedback, DeepSeek's user interface includes notifications and alerts that keep users informed of their progress. Whether it's a successful data upload, an error message, or the completion of an analysis, these alerts appear prominently on the screen. This feature ensures that users are always aware of the current status of their projects and can make informed decisions without unnecessary delays. Additionally, a help icon is readily accessible, offering guidance and tutorials for those who may encounter challenges while navigating the interface.

Finally, user settings can be accessed through the main navigation bar, allowing individuals to personalize their experience. Users can adjust preferences such as notification settings, theme options, and accessibility features to suit their needs. This level of customization is vital for creating an inclusive environment where every user can feel comfortable and confident while using DeepSeek. By mastering the user interface, users can unlock the full potential of this powerful AI tool, making significant strides in their projects and gaining valuable insights into their data.

Chapter 3: Core Features of DeepSeek

Data Input and Management

Data input and management are critical components in harnessing the full potential of AI tools like DeepSeek. Users must understand the various methods of inputting data into the system to ensure accurate and efficient processing. DeepSeek supports multiple data formats, including text files, images, and structured data from databases. Understanding these formats and the types of data that can be effectively utilized will help users maximize the tool's capabilities. Proper data input not only enhances the performance of the AI but also ensures that the outcomes are relevant and actionable, aligning with users' goals.

Once the data has been inputted into DeepSeek, effective management becomes paramount. Users need to categorize and organize their data systematically. This involves labeling data points, creating metadata, and utilizing tagging systems that make it easier to retrieve and analyze information later. By establishing a clear framework for data management, users can streamline their workflows, reduce redundancy, and enhance collaboration when working in teams. A well-structured data management system ensures that users can quickly locate the necessary data for their projects, which is crucial for maintaining productivity and efficiency.

Another significant aspect of data management is the process of data cleaning and preprocessing. Raw data often contains errors, inconsistencies, or irrelevant information that can lead to inaccurate results. Users must familiarize themselves with techniques for cleaning their data, such as removing duplicates, correcting errors, and standardizing formats. DeepSeek provides tools that assist in this process, helping users to automate certain tasks and focus on more complex data management challenges. By prioritizing data quality, users can improve the reliability of the AI's outputs, making their insights more trustworthy and impactful.

Additionally, users should be aware of the importance of data security and privacy. With increasing concerns about data breaches and unauthorized access, it is essential to implement robust security measures when managing sensitive information. DeepSeek offers various security features, including encryption and user access controls, to help users protect their data. Understanding the implications of data privacy regulations, such as GDPR or CCPA, is also crucial. Users need to ensure that their data management practices comply with these regulations to avoid potential legal issues and maintain user trust.

Finally, ongoing monitoring and evaluation of data input and management practices are vital for continuous improvement. Users should regularly assess their data management strategies to identify areas for enhancement. This could include adopting new technologies or methods for data storage and retrieval. DeepSeek encourages users to share their experiences and best practices within the community, fostering a collaborative environment that drives innovation. By remaining adaptable and open to change, users can ensure that their data management practices evolve alongside advancements in AI technology, ultimately maximizing the benefits of using DeepSeek.

Analyzing Data with DeepSeek

Analyzing data with DeepSeek involves leveraging its advanced algorithms to extract meaningful insights from vast datasets. The tool is designed to streamline the data analysis process, making it accessible even for those new to artificial intelligence. Users can begin by uploading their datasets, which can include structured, semi-structured, or unstructured data. DeepSeek supports various file formats, allowing for a seamless integration of data from multiple sources. Once the data is loaded, users can explore its features and characteristics through a user-friendly interface that simplifies the initial steps of analysis.

One of the standout features of DeepSeek is its intuitive data visualization capabilities. Users can transform complex data into visual representations that facilitate easier understanding and interpretation. Charts, graphs, and heat maps are among the visualization tools available, enabling users to identify patterns, trends, and anomalies quickly. This functionality is particularly beneficial for beginners who may not have extensive experience in data analytics but wish to gain insights from their data without getting lost in technical jargon or complicated methodologies.

DeepSeek also incorporates powerful machine learning algorithms that enhance the analysis process. Users can apply these algorithms to their datasets to uncover hidden relationships and predictive insights. The platform allows for clustering, classification, and regression analysis, providing users with a comprehensive toolkit for data exploration. By utilizing these advanced techniques, users can derive actionable insights that may have remained obscured through traditional analysis methods. Additionally, DeepSeek's automated features reduce the time and effort required for data preparation, enabling users to focus on interpreting results instead.

Collaboration is another key aspect of using DeepSeek for data analysis. The platform supports team efforts by allowing multiple users to share projects and insights easily. This collaborative environment fosters ideation and diverse perspectives, enhancing the quality of the analysis. Users can annotate findings, share visualizations, and collaborate in real-time, making it an ideal choice for teams working on data-driven projects. Such features ensure that insights are not only derived but also effectively communicated among team members, leading to more informed decision-making.

Finally, an important consideration when analyzing data with DeepSeek is the ethical implications of AI-driven analysis. Users must remain aware of data privacy and the potential biases that can arise from algorithmic processing. DeepSeek provides tools and guidelines to help users navigate these issues, encouraging responsible usage of AI technologies. By fostering a culture of ethical analysis, users can maximize the benefits of DeepSeek while contributing positively to the broader landscape of data science and AI. This focus on ethics complements the technical capabilities of the platform, ensuring that users are equipped to harness the power of AI responsibly and effectively.

Visualizing Results

Visualizing results is a crucial step in the process of leveraging AI tools like DeepSeek. As users engage with this powerful software, understanding how to effectively interpret and present the outcomes of their analyses can significantly enhance decision-making and strategy development. Visualization transforms complex data sets into understandable formats, enabling users to identify patterns, trends, and insights that may not be immediately apparent through raw data alone. This subchapter will explore various techniques and tools available within DeepSeek to help users visualize their results effectively.

One of the primary visualization techniques available in DeepSeek is the use of graphs and charts. These visual representations allow for quick comparisons and highlight key metrics that can influence business strategies. Users can generate bar charts, line graphs, and pie charts to represent different aspects of their data, making it easier to digest. For instance, a line graph can effectively showcase trends over time, while a pie chart can illustrate the proportionate distribution of categories. Understanding which type of visualization to use in different scenarios is essential for maximizing the insights gained from the data.

In addition to basic charts, DeepSeek offers more advanced visualization options, such as heat maps and scatter plots. Heat maps are particularly useful for displaying data density, allowing users to identify areas of high concentration at a glance. Scatter plots can reveal correlations between variables, helping users to understand relationships that may be present in their data. By incorporating these advanced visualization techniques, users can deepen their analysis and gain a more nuanced understanding of their results, which can lead to more informed decisions.

Furthermore, integrating visualizations into reports and presentations is vital for communicating findings effectively. DeepSeek allows users to export visualizations in various formats, ensuring compatibility with popular presentation software and reporting tools. This feature enhances the ability of users to share insights with stakeholders and team members, fostering collaboration and informed discussions. By presenting visualized results, users can engage their audience more effectively, making complex data more accessible and actionable.

Lastly, users should consider the importance of interactivity in visualizations. DeepSeek includes interactive visualization tools that allow users to explore data dynamically. This interactivity can facilitate deeper investigation and enable users to manipulate variables to see how changes affect outcomes. By providing stakeholders with interactive dashboards, users can empower their teams to conduct their analyses, fostering a culture of data-driven decision-making. This approach not only enhances understanding but also encourages a more hands-on engagement with the data and results, ultimately leading to more strategic insights.

Chapter 4: Basic Functions of DeepSeek

Running Basic Queries

Running basic queries in DeepSeek is a crucial step for users looking to harness the full potential of this powerful AI tool. Understanding how to construct and execute these queries allows users to extract relevant information efficiently. Basic queries serve as the foundation for more advanced data retrieval strategies and enable users to interact intuitively with the platform. By mastering these fundamental skills, users can enhance their productivity and gain deeper insights into their datasets.

To start, users should familiarize themselves with the query interface of DeepSeek. The interface is designed to be user-friendly, allowing for straightforward input of queries. Users can begin with simple keyword searches, entering one or more terms related to the information they seek. This basic approach can yield immediate results, showcasing the breadth of data available within the system. Additionally, users can refine their searches by utilizing filters such as date ranges, categories, or specific data types, which can significantly narrow down the results for more relevant output.

As users gain confidence in executing basic queries, they can explore more complex query structures. This involves using operators such as AND, OR, and NOT to combine multiple keywords and phrases effectively. For example, a query that seeks information on "machine learning" AND "data science" will return results that include both terms, allowing for a more targeted approach. Understanding these operators not only enhances the specificity of searches but also broadens the range of potential insights that users can uncover.

Furthermore, DeepSeek supports natural language processing, enabling users to formulate queries in plain language. This feature is particularly beneficial for those who may not be familiar with technical query syntax. Users can simply ask questions or make statements, and DeepSeek will interpret these inputs to provide relevant results. This capability empowers users to engage with the tool more intuitively, making it accessible to a wider audience, including those without a background in data analysis.

Finally, users should take advantage of the query history feature in DeepSeek. This tool allows users to review previous queries and results, making it easier to refine searches and revisit past findings. By analyzing their query history, users can identify patterns in their search behaviors and adjust their strategies accordingly. Overall, running basic queries in DeepSeek is an essential skill that lays the groundwork for more advanced data exploration, enabling users to leverage AI capabilities effectively and efficiently.

Understanding Output Formats

Output formats in AI tools like DeepSeek play a crucial role in determining how users can interpret and utilize the results generated by the system. Understanding these formats is essential for maximizing the potential of DeepSeek, as it allows users to tailor their interactions with the tool to suit specific needs. Output formats can include text, images, charts, and more, each serving different purposes based on the type of data generated and the user's objectives.

Text output is one of the most common formats provided by AI tools. In DeepSeek, text output can range from simple summaries to detailed reports. This format is particularly useful for users who need to distill complex information into understandable insights. The challenge for users lies in interpreting these outputs in context, ensuring that the generated text aligns with the queries made and the data analyzed. Familiarity with the nuances of text output can significantly enhance a user's ability to draw meaningful conclusions from the results.

In addition to text, DeepSeek can generate visual outputs, such as charts and graphs. These formats are particularly valuable when dealing with large datasets, as they allow for quick visual assessments of trends and patterns. Users can benefit from understanding how to read and interpret these visual formats to extract actionable insights. Furthermore, visual outputs can often convey information more effectively than text alone, making them an essential component of data analysis in DeepSeek.

Another important output format is structured data, often presented in tables or spreadsheets. This format is ideal for users who need to perform further analysis or integrate the results into other applications. Understanding how to manipulate and utilize structured data can significantly enhance a user's workflow. DeepSeek's ability to export results in this format enables users to leverage powerful data analysis tools, fostering a more in-depth exploration of the insights generated by the AI.

Lastly, users should be aware of the potential for custom output formats in DeepSeek. The ability to customize outputs to meet specific requirements can greatly enhance the user experience. This flexibility allows users to define how they want their results to be presented, ensuring that the information is not only useful but also aligned with their individual needs. By understanding and leveraging the various output formats available in DeepSeek, users can unlock the full potential of this powerful AI tool, transforming raw data into valuable insights with ease.

Exporting Results

Exporting results is a crucial aspect of utilizing DeepSeek, enabling users to effectively leverage the insights gained from their AI analyses. This functionality allows users to transfer their findings into formats that are compatible with other applications or for sharing purposes. Understanding how to export results efficiently can enhance collaboration and streamline workflows, making it easier to integrate AI-generated insights into broader projects or presentations.

DeepSeek offers various options for exporting results, catering to different user needs and preferences. Users can choose from formats such as CSV, JSON, or even visual representations like charts and graphs. Each format serves a specific purpose; for example, CSV files are ideal for data analysis and manipulation in spreadsheet software, while JSON is useful for developers who want to integrate the output into web applications or databases. Knowing the right format to use can significantly impact how results are utilized in subsequent tasks.

The process of exporting results in DeepSeek is designed to be user-friendly. Users can easily navigate through the interface to select the desired output format and specify the parameters for their export. This includes defining which data fields to include, filtering results based on certain criteria, and organizing the output for clarity. By taking advantage of these options, users can tailor the exported data to their specific needs, ensuring that the results are both relevant and actionable.

In addition to standard export options, DeepSeek also provides functionality for automation. Users can set up scheduled exports, allowing data to be generated and exported at regular intervals without manual intervention. This feature is particularly beneficial for ongoing projects or monitoring tasks where timely updates are essential. Automation not only saves time but also minimizes the risk of human error, ensuring that the data remains consistent and reliable.

Finally, it's important for users to consider the implications of sharing exported results. Whether for collaboration with team members or presentation to stakeholders, understanding the context and significance of the data is essential. Users should also pay attention to data privacy and security, especially when handling sensitive information. By exporting results thoughtfully and responsibly, users can maximize the impact of their findings while maintaining ethical standards in data management.

Chapter 5: DeepSeek in Action

Case Study: Using DeepSeek for Market Analysis

In the realm of market analysis, DeepSeek has emerged as a transformative tool that empowers users to harness the power of artificial intelligence effectively. This case study examines how a mid-sized retail company implemented DeepSeek to enhance its market analysis capabilities. The company faced challenges in understanding consumer behavior, identifying market trends, and making data-driven decisions. By leveraging DeepSeek's advanced data processing algorithms, the firm was able to streamline its analysis process and uncover insights that were previously difficult to obtain.

The initial step in the implementation of DeepSeek involved integrating the tool with the company's existing databases. This allowed the AI platform to access a wealth of historical sales data, customer feedback, and market trends. Once integrated, the company utilized DeepSeek's unique algorithms to analyze patterns in consumer purchasing behavior. The AI was able to sift through vast amounts of unstructured data, identifying correlations and trends that manual analysis had overlooked. This level of analysis not only saved time but also provided a depth of insight that significantly informed the company's strategic planning.

One of the most notable outcomes of using DeepSeek was the identification of emerging market trends. The AI tool detected shifts in consumer preferences, highlighting a growing demand for sustainable products. Through detailed reports generated by DeepSeek, the retail company was able to pivot its inventory strategy, introducing eco-friendly products that aligned with consumer demand. This proactive approach not only enhanced customer satisfaction but also positioned the company as a leader in sustainability within its industry, illustrating the value of data-driven decision-making.

Furthermore, DeepSeek's predictive analytics capabilities allowed the company to forecast future sales trends with greater accuracy. By analyzing historical data alongside current market indicators, the AI tool provided actionable insights that informed marketing strategies and promotional campaigns. This predictive accuracy meant that the company could allocate resources more effectively, reducing waste and optimizing operational efficiency. As a result, the firm experienced not only improved sales performance but also an enhanced return on investment in its marketing initiatives.

In conclusion, the case study of the retail company exemplifies the profound impact of using DeepSeek for market analysis. By integrating this powerful AI tool into their operations, the company was able to unlock valuable insights that drove strategic decision-making. The success achieved through DeepSeek underscores the importance of embracing advanced technologies in today's competitive market landscape. As users continue to explore the potential of DeepSeek, the insights gained will undoubtedly empower them to navigate their respective markets with confidence and foresight.

Case Study: DeepSeek for Academic Research

DeepSeek has emerged as a transformative tool for academic research, enabling scholars to leverage artificial intelligence for enhanced data analysis and knowledge discovery. This case study presents an in-depth look at how researchers in various fields have utilized DeepSeek to streamline their workflows, improve data accessibility, and facilitate innovative research methodologies. By applying AI-driven algorithms, DeepSeek assists users in overcoming traditional challenges associated with data management and literature review, making it an indispensable asset in the academic landscape.

One notable example of DeepSeek's application is in the field of biomedical research, where researchers often face an overwhelming amount of literature. A team at a university utilized DeepSeek to automate their literature review process. By inputting specific keywords and parameters related to their research on cancer therapies, they were able to quickly identify and categorize thousands of relevant studies. DeepSeek not only reduced the time spent on manual searches but also improved the comprehensiveness of their literature review, ultimately enhancing the quality of their research findings.

In the humanities, DeepSeek has been instrumental in assisting researchers with text analysis and interpretation. A group of historians employed the tool to analyze historical texts, looking for patterns and themes that might not be readily apparent through traditional reading methods. By using DeepSeek's advanced natural language processing capabilities, they could uncover connections across different texts and time periods, leading to new insights and interpretations that contributed significantly to their research. This case highlights how DeepSeek empowers researchers to go beyond surface-level analysis and engage in deeper scholarly inquiry.

Social sciences have also benefited from DeepSeek's capabilities, particularly in the realm of survey data analysis. Researchers conducting large-scale surveys found the tool invaluable for managing and interpreting complex data sets. By utilizing DeepSeek's machine learning algorithms, they could identify trends and correlations within the data that informed their hypotheses and conclusions. This not only enhanced the robustness of their findings but also allowed for more nuanced discussions about social behavior and policy implications, showcasing DeepSeek's versatility across diverse academic disciplines.

Overall, the case study of DeepSeek in academic research illustrates its powerful impact on improving efficiency and enriching the research process. As scholars continue to grapple with vast amounts of information and the necessity for rigorous analysis, tools like DeepSeek are becoming essential. By integrating AI into their research methodologies, academics can unlock new potentials in discovering knowledge, ultimately advancing their fields and contributing to the broader academic community.

Case Study: Implementing DeepSeek in Business

Implementing DeepSeek in a business context can provide significant advantages, particularly in sectors driven by data analysis and customer engagement. A notable case study involves a mid-sized e-commerce company that sought to enhance its product recommendation system. By integrating DeepSeek into its existing infrastructure, the company aimed to leverage AI capabilities to analyze customer behavior more effectively and improve sales conversions. The results of this implementation offer valuable insights into the practical benefits and challenges of using DeepSeek in a business environment.

Initially, the company conducted a thorough assessment of its data landscape. This involved gathering information from various sources, including customer interactions, purchase history, and browsing patterns. DeepSeek's advanced algorithms were utilized to process this data, identifying trends and preferences among different customer segments. The integration process included training the AI model on historical data to ensure it could make accurate predictions about future customer behavior. This foundational step was critical in setting up a robust recommendation engine that could deliver personalized experiences to users.

Once the model was trained, the company implemented the recommendations generated by DeepSeek directly onto its platform. Customers began to see tailored product suggestions based on their individual preferences and previous interactions. The initial results were impressive, showing a 20% increase in click-through rates on recommended products. This increase not only improved customer satisfaction but also led to a noticeable rise in overall sales. The personalized approach transformed how customers engaged with the e-commerce site, illustrating the power of AI in enhancing user experience.

However, the implementation of DeepSeek was not without its challenges. The company faced difficulties in ensuring data quality and relevance, as inconsistent or outdated data could skew the AI's recommendations. To address this, ongoing data management practices were established, including regular audits and updates to the data sets used for training the model. Additionally, the company invested in staff training to enhance understanding of how to interpret and act on the insights generated by DeepSeek. These steps were crucial for maintaining the effectiveness of the AI tool and maximizing its potential.

In conclusion, the case study of the e-commerce company illustrates the transformative potential of implementing DeepSeek in a business setting. By effectively harnessing AI capabilities, the company not only improved its product recommendations but also fostered a deeper connection with its customers. The experience highlights the importance of careful planning, data management, and staff training when integrating AI tools like DeepSeek. For other businesses considering similar implementations, this case study serves as a valuable reference point for understanding both the opportunities and challenges associated with adopting AI technologies.

Chapter 6: Advanced Techniques

Customizing Queries

Customizing queries in DeepSeek is essential for users who want to maximize the effectiveness of their AI interactions. By tailoring your queries, you can extract more relevant and precise information from the AI, ensuring that the responses align with your specific needs. The customization process allows users to refine their search parameters, making it easier to navigate vast amounts of data and obtain insights that are not only accurate but also contextually relevant. Understanding how to structure and modify queries can significantly enhance the overall user experience with the AI tool.

One of the fundamental aspects of customizing queries is the use of keywords. Keywords act as the backbone of your query, directing the AI to focus on particular concepts or topics. Users should select keywords carefully, considering synonyms and related terms that might yield additional information. For instance, if you are searching for insights on "machine learning," incorporating related phrases like "artificial intelligence" or "deep learning" can broaden the scope of results. Experimenting with different keywords can help identify the most effective combinations for retrieving the desired information.

Another important technique for customizing queries is the use of filters. Filters allow users to narrow down their search results based on specific criteria. DeepSeek offers various filtering options, such as date ranges, content types, and relevance scores. By applying these filters, users can eliminate irrelevant results and focus on the most pertinent information. For example, if you are looking for recent advancements in AI, applying a date filter will ensure that you only receive information that is current and applicable. This not only saves time but also enhances the quality of the results.

Additionally, users can leverage the power of natural language processing (NLP) to customize their queries. DeepSeek's NLP capabilities enable users to ask questions in a more conversational manner, allowing for a more intuitive interaction with the AI. This means that instead of formulating queries in a rigid format, users can phrase their inquiries as they would in a normal conversation. This flexibility can lead to improved understanding and more relevant responses, as the AI can better interpret the context and intent behind the query.

Finally, iterating on your queries is a key practice for effective customization. After receiving initial responses from DeepSeek, users should assess the results critically. If the information provided does not meet expectations, consider adjusting the query by modifying keywords, applying different filters, or rephrasing questions. This iterative process allows for continuous improvement in the quality of information retrieved. Over time, users will develop a deeper understanding of how to customize their queries effectively, leading to more insightful and actionable outcomes.

Integrating DeepSeek with Other Tools

Integrating DeepSeek with other tools can significantly enhance its capabilities and streamline various workflows. DeepSeek is designed to be versatile, allowing users to connect it with a range of applications that can complement its functionalities. This integration can help users automate repetitive tasks, analyze data more effectively, and leverage existing tools in their operations. Understanding how to bring together DeepSeek with other software can empower users to maximize their productivity and harness the full potential of artificial intelligence.

One of the key integrations users may consider is connecting DeepSeek with data visualization tools. By exporting data insights generated by DeepSeek into platforms like Tableau or Power BI, users can create compelling visual representations of their findings. This not only aids in better understanding complex datasets but also makes it easier to communicate insights to stakeholders. The combination of DeepSeek's analytical prowess and visualization tools can lead to more informed decision-making and strategic planning.

Additionally, integrating DeepSeek with project management software can enhance collaboration within teams. Tools like Trello or Asana can be linked to DeepSeek, enabling users to assign tasks based on AI-generated insights. For instance, if DeepSeek identifies a trend that requires immediate attention, a task can be automatically created, assigned, and tracked within the project management tool. This seamless connection allows teams to respond quickly to insights and align their efforts more effectively, thereby improving overall project outcomes.

Another valuable integration is with customer relationship management (CRM) systems. By connecting DeepSeek to platforms such as Salesforce or HubSpot, users can gain deeper insights into customer behavior and preferences. DeepSeek can analyze customer data, identify patterns, and provide recommendations for engagement strategies. This enriched understanding enables businesses to tailor their marketing and sales efforts, ultimately leading to improved customer relationships and increased revenue.

Lastly, integrating DeepSeek with communication tools can enhance team collaboration further. Connecting DeepSeek with platforms like Slack or Microsoft Teams can facilitate real-time sharing of insights and updates. Users can set up notifications for when certain thresholds are met or when significant trends are detected, allowing teams to stay informed without needing to constantly monitor DeepSeek. This integration fosters a culture of responsiveness and agility, helping teams to pivot quickly based on the latest data-driven insights.

Troubleshooting Common Issues

When using DeepSeek, users may encounter various issues that can impede their progress. Understanding how to troubleshoot these common problems is essential for maximizing the effectiveness of this powerful AI tool. This subchapter will address some of the typical challenges users face and provide practical solutions to help overcome them.

One common issue is slow processing times. Users may experience delays when running queries or generating results. To address this, it is advisable to check the internet connection, as a weak or unstable connection can significantly affect performance. Additionally, users should ensure that their system meets the required specifications for running DeepSeek efficiently. Closing unnecessary applications and clearing cache can also help improve performance.

Another frequent concern is the accuracy of results. Users may find that the outputs do not align with their expectations or are not relevant to their queries. This can often be attributed to poorly formulated queries. To enhance accuracy, users should refine their input by using more specific keywords and phrases. Utilizing the advanced filtering options available in DeepSeek can also help narrow down results to better match user intent.

Users might also face issues with account access and permissions. Problems such as being locked out of an account or encountering permission errors can disrupt workflow. In such cases, users should first attempt to reset their passwords or check their account status. If the problem persists, contacting customer support is advisable, as they can provide assistance in resolving access-related issues promptly.

Lastly, integration challenges with other tools and platforms can arise when using DeepSeek. Users may find difficulties in syncing data or exporting results to external applications. To troubleshoot this, ensuring that all software is updated to the latest versions is crucial. Users should also consult the integration guidelines provided by DeepSeek, as these resources can offer insights into compatible formats and settings necessary for successful interoperability.

Chapter 7: Best Practices for DeepSeek Users

Effective Data Management

Effective data management is essential for harnessing the full potential of DeepSeek, a powerful AI tool designed to streamline data processing and enhance decision-making. Data management encompasses a variety of practices and processes that ensure data is accurate, accessible, and secure. Users must implement effective data management strategies to maintain the integrity of their datasets and facilitate efficient AI operations. This subchapter will guide users through the key components of data management, including data organization, storage solutions, data quality assurance, and compliance with data regulations.

One of the foundational aspects of effective data management is data organization. Users should categorize their data systematically, using clear naming conventions and folder structures. This organization aids in the retrieval and analysis of data, allowing users to quickly find the information they need. Utilizing metadata can further enhance organization by providing context and details about the dataset, such as creation date and data source. Tools within DeepSeek can assist in tagging and categorizing data, making it easier for users to manage large volumes of information efficiently.

Storage solutions play a critical role in data management as well. Users must evaluate their storage options based on their data volume, access requirements, and budget constraints. Cloud storage offers flexibility and scalability, allowing users to store and access data from virtually anywhere. On the other hand, local storage may provide faster access speeds for certain applications but could limit scalability. DeepSeek integrates with various storage solutions, enabling users to choose the best option that aligns with their operational needs while ensuring data security and reliability.

Ensuring data quality is another vital component of effective data management. Users should regularly implement data validation techniques to check for inaccuracies, duplicates, and inconsistencies within their datasets. Establishing data governance practices, such as defining data ownership and accountability, can help maintain high data quality standards. DeepSeek features tools that assist in identifying and rectifying data quality issues, allowing users to trust the insights generated by the AI tool. High-quality data is crucial for making informed decisions, and users must prioritize this aspect to maximize DeepSeek's capabilities.

Compliance with data regulations is an increasingly important consideration for users managing data. With various regulations in place, such as GDPR and CCPA, users must ensure that their data management practices adhere to legal requirements. This includes implementing measures for data protection, privacy, and ethical data usage. DeepSeek provides resources and guidance to help users navigate these regulations, ensuring that their data practices are compliant and responsible. By prioritizing compliance, users not only protect their organizations from potential legal issues but also build trust with their clients and stakeholders.

In conclusion, effective data management is a critical foundation for maximizing the potential of DeepSeek. By focusing on data organization, selecting appropriate storage solutions, ensuring data quality, and adhering to compliance regulations, users can create an environment conducive to data-driven decision-making. As users master these data management strategies, they will be better equipped to leverage the powerful capabilities of DeepSeek, unlocking new opportunities for innovation and efficiency in their respective fields.

Maintaining Data Integrity

Maintaining data integrity is crucial for maximizing the potential of DeepSeek, as the accuracy and consistency of your data directly influence the outcomes of your AI applications. Data integrity refers to the correctness and reliability of data throughout its lifecycle. When using DeepSeek, maintaining high data integrity ensures that the insights generated are trustworthy and actionable. Users must adopt specific practices to safeguard their data from corruption, loss, or unauthorized access, which can significantly hinder the effectiveness of AI-driven analyses.

One key aspect of maintaining data integrity is ensuring accurate data entry. Users should implement validation checks at the point of data collection to minimize errors. This can involve using automated tools that flag inconsistencies or duplicate entries before the data is loaded into DeepSeek. Additionally, training team members on best practices for data entry can help reduce human errors. Consistent formatting and standardized procedures for data input are also essential in establishing a reliable dataset that DeepSeek can analyze effectively.

Another important factor is regular data audits. Users should conduct periodic reviews of their datasets to identify and rectify any discrepancies or anomalies. These audits can help detect issues such as outdated information, missing values, or unintentional alterations. Establishing a schedule for these audits and employing automated tools can streamline the process, allowing users to maintain a high level of data integrity without significant manual intervention. Keeping a log of changes made during audits can also provide a useful reference, helping to track the evolution of the dataset over time.

Data security is a critical component of data integrity as well. Users must implement security measures to protect their data from unauthorized access, which can compromise data integrity. This includes setting strong passwords, using encryption for sensitive information, and restricting access to data based on user roles. Regularly updating security protocols and software can also help safeguard data against evolving threats. By prioritizing data security, users can protect the integrity of their datasets, ensuring that DeepSeek operates on the most reliable information available.

Lastly, fostering a culture of data stewardship within organizations is vital for maintaining data integrity. Users should encourage open communication about data management practices and promote accountability among team members. Providing training sessions and resources on data integrity best practices can empower users to take ownership of their data. By instilling a sense of responsibility regarding data accuracy and security, organizations can create an environment where data integrity is a shared priority, ultimately enhancing the effectiveness of DeepSeek and the insights it provides.

Continuous Learning and Improvement

Continuous learning and improvement are essential components for users seeking to maximize their experience with DeepSeek. As a powerful AI tool, DeepSeek operates in a dynamic environment where data, user needs, and technological advancements are constantly evolving. To stay ahead, users must adopt a mindset that embraces ongoing education and adaptation. This not only enhances personal proficiency but also optimizes the overall efficiency and effectiveness of the AI tool in various applications.

One effective approach to continuous learning is through regular training and workshops. Many organizations offer resources, including webinars and interactive sessions, that cover new features, best practices, and case studies. Engaging in these opportunities allows users to deepen their understanding of DeepSeek's capabilities and discover innovative ways to apply the tool in their specific contexts. Additionally, users can benefit from networking with peers who are facing similar challenges, fostering a collaborative environment for sharing insights and solutions.

Feedback plays a crucial role in the learning process. Users are encouraged to provide input on their experiences with DeepSeek, whether through formal surveys or informal discussions. This feedback not only helps developers to enhance the tool but also allows users to reflect on their own usage patterns and identify areas for improvement. By taking an active role in the feedback loop, users not only contribute to the evolution of DeepSeek but also gain a deeper understanding of their own needs and how to address them effectively.

Another key aspect of continuous learning is staying informed about industry trends and advancements in artificial intelligence. Subscribing to relevant newsletters, following thought leaders on social media, and participating in online forums can provide valuable insights. Understanding the broader landscape of AI can help users anticipate changes, adapt their strategies, and leverage DeepSeek in ways that align with emerging best practices. This proactive approach enables users to maintain a competitive edge and harness the full potential of the tool.

Finally, users should cultivate a habit of self-reflection and goal-setting. Regularly assessing their skills and knowledge related to DeepSeek allows users to identify gaps and set tangible goals for improvement. Establishing a routine for learning, whether through dedicated study time or practical experimentation with the tool, reinforces a culture of continuous improvement. By committing to lifelong learning, users can ensure that they not only keep pace with the advancements in AI but also harness the full capabilities of DeepSeek to achieve their objectives.

Chapter 8: Future Trends in AI and DeepSeek

Upcoming Features in DeepSeek

DeepSeek is continuously evolving, and several upcoming features are set to enhance user experience and expand functionality. One of the most anticipated features is the integration of advanced natural language processing capabilities. This will allow users to interact with the platform more intuitively, enabling them to input queries in a conversational manner. The goal is to make DeepSeek more accessible, especially for those who may not be familiar with technical jargon or complex terminology. This enhancement will streamline the user experience, making it easier to extract valuable insights from vast datasets.

Another significant addition is the enhanced data visualization tools. Users will soon be able to create dynamic visual representations of their data, including interactive graphs, charts, and maps. These tools will not only help users analyze data more effectively but will also facilitate better presentations of findings. By transforming complex data sets into visually appealing graphics, users can communicate insights more clearly to stakeholders, making their reports more impactful and easier to understand.

DeepSeek is also focusing on expanding its integration capabilities with other software tools. The upcoming feature set will include seamless connectivity with popular platforms used in various industries, such as CRM systems, project management tools, and data analytics applications. This integration will allow users to pull data from multiple sources into DeepSeek, providing a comprehensive view of their information landscape. As a result, users will be able to perform more in-depth analyses without the need for manual data consolidation, thereby saving time and reducing the risk of errors.

Security and privacy enhancements are also on the horizon. With the increasing importance of data protection, DeepSeek is prioritizing user security by implementing advanced encryption protocols and user authentication processes. These features will ensure that sensitive data remains protected and that users can trust the platform with their information. The commitment to safeguarding user data is critical, especially for professionals handling confidential or proprietary information in their organizations.

Lastly, DeepSeek plans to introduce a personalized recommendation engine that will suggest tailored insights and actions based on user behavior and preferences. This feature aims to make the platform smarter, providing users with proactive guidance on how best to leverage their data. By analyzing user interactions and identifying patterns, the recommendation engine will help users discover new opportunities and optimize their workflows, ultimately enhancing productivity and decision-making processes. As these features roll out, users can expect a more robust and user-friendly experience with DeepSeek.

The Future of AI Tools

The future of AI tools, particularly in the context of platforms like DeepSeek, is poised for significant evolution. As technology continues to advance, users can expect AI tools to become increasingly sophisticated, offering enhanced capabilities that streamline workflows and improve overall efficiency. These tools will likely integrate more seamlessly with existing systems, allowing users to harness their full potential without extensive training. The focus will shift toward creating intuitive interfaces that cater to both novice and experienced users, making AI more accessible than ever.

One of the most promising areas for AI tool development is natural language processing (NLP). As NLP technology improves, AI tools will become better at understanding and generating human language, enabling more effective communication between users and machines. This enhancement will facilitate tasks such as content generation, data analysis, and customer support, allowing users to interact with AI tools in a more conversational manner. As a result, users will find it easier to delegate tasks to AI, freeing up valuable time for more strategic activities.

Furthermore, the integration of AI tools with other technologies will likely lead to the creation of interconnected ecosystems. For instance, DeepSeek could incorporate machine learning algorithms that adapt to user behavior over time, offering personalized recommendations and insights. This level of customization will empower users to maximize their productivity by tailoring the AI's functionality to their specific needs. As these ecosystems evolve, users will benefit from a more holistic approach to task management and decision-making.

Data privacy and ethical considerations will also shape the future of AI tools. As AI becomes more prevalent in various industries, users will demand greater transparency regarding how their data is used and processed. This demand will push developers to implement robust security measures and ethical guidelines in their AI tools. Users can expect to see features that allow them to control their data, ensuring that their privacy is respected while still benefiting from AI-driven insights and automation.

Lastly, ongoing advancements in AI research will continue to drive innovation in AI tools like DeepSeek. As researchers discover new algorithms and techniques, users will benefit from features that were previously unimaginable. These advancements will open new avenues for creativity and problem-solving, encouraging users to explore novel applications of AI in their work. The future of AI tools promises to be dynamic and transformative, offering users the opportunity to unlock their full potential in ways that enhance productivity and creativity.

Preparing for Changes in Technology

Preparing for changes in technology is essential for users aiming to master DeepSeek and harness its full potential. As artificial intelligence continues to evolve, the tools and methodologies associated with it also undergo significant transformations. Understanding these changes allows users to stay ahead and maximize their proficiency with AI tools like DeepSeek. This preparation involves not only adapting to new features and updates but also cultivating a mindset that embraces continuous learning and flexibility.

One of the first steps in preparing for technological changes is to stay informed about the latest developments in AI and DeepSeek specifically. Regularly following updates from official sources, such as the DeepSeek website, blogs, and community forums, can provide valuable insights into new functionalities, enhancements, and best practices. Engaging with industry news and trends further equips users with the knowledge necessary to adapt their strategies and workflows. This proactive approach ensures that users do not become stagnant but rather evolve alongside the technology.

Additionally, users should invest time in training and educational resources that deepen their understanding of AI concepts and tools. Many platforms offer tutorials, webinars, and online courses tailored to various skill levels. By taking advantage of these resources, users can build a robust foundation in AI principles, enhancing their ability to navigate DeepSeek effectively. This commitment to ongoing education will not only facilitate smoother transitions during technological updates but also empower users to leverage new capabilities confidently.

Another critical aspect of preparing for changes in technology is fostering a culture of experimentation and adaptability. Users should be encouraged to explore new features and functionalities as they are released, testing them in real-world scenarios. This hands-on approach not only solidifies learning but also uncovers unique ways to apply DeepSeek to specific tasks or projects. Embracing a mindset that welcomes trial and error can lead to innovative solutions and a deeper appreciation for the tool's capabilities.

Lastly, collaborating with peers and participating in user communities can significantly enhance the preparation process. By sharing experiences, challenges, and solutions, users can learn from one another and collectively adapt to changes in technology. These interactions often lead to the discovery of best practices and shortcuts that may not be evident in formal training. Building a network of fellow users provides a support system that can help individuals navigate the complexities of DeepSeek and AI technology, ultimately leading to a more enriched user experience.

Chapter 9: Additional Resources

Online Communities and Forums

Online communities and forums have become essential platforms for users seeking to enhance their knowledge and skills in various fields, including artificial intelligence. For those interested in mastering DeepSeek, these digital spaces offer a wealth of information, support, and networking opportunities. Engaging with like-minded individuals can significantly accelerate the learning process, as users share their experiences, challenges, and successes. The collaborative nature of these communities fosters an environment where beginners can ask questions, seek advice, and gain insights that may not be readily available in traditional educational resources.

Forums dedicated to AI and specifically to tools like DeepSeek often feature a variety of topics, ranging from basic usage tips to advanced techniques. Users can find threads discussing specific functionalities of DeepSeek, troubleshooting common issues, and exploring best practices for maximizing the tool's potential. The diversity of content available helps users at all levels, whether they are just starting or looking to deepen their understanding. This vast repository of knowledge contributes to a more comprehensive grasp of AI applications and encourages experimentation and innovation among users.

Participating actively in online communities not only enhances individual learning but also builds a sense of belonging. When users contribute to discussions, share their projects, or provide feedback on others' work, they create connections that can lead to collaborative projects and partnerships. This networking aspect is particularly valuable in the fast-evolving field of AI, where sharing insights and resources can lead to new ideas and advancements. By engaging with others, users can also stay updated on the latest trends, tools, and updates related to DeepSeek and the broader AI landscape.

Moreover, online forums often host events such as webinars, workshops, and challenges that provide hands-on experience with DeepSeek. These opportunities allow users to apply their knowledge in practical scenarios, reinforcing learning through action. By participating in these events, users can also interact directly with experts and seasoned practitioners, gaining perspectives that can be transformative for their understanding of AI tools. Such experiences not only enhance individual skills but also contribute to the overall growth of the community, as members share their learnings and outcomes.

In conclusion, online communities and forums serve as invaluable resources for users looking to master DeepSeek and explore the realm of artificial intelligence. By tapping into the collective knowledge and experiences of others, users can navigate their learning paths more effectively. The supportive and collaborative nature of these platforms encourages continuous growth, making them an essential element of the journey towards unlocking the full potential of AI tools like DeepSeek. As users engage with these communities, they not only enhance their own skills but also contribute to a vibrant ecosystem that fosters innovation and discovery in AI applications.

Recommended Reading

In the journey of mastering DeepSeek, a variety of resources can enhance your understanding and application of this powerful AI tool. Recommended reading materials span from foundational texts to contemporary analyses, providing a comprehensive view of AI technologies and their practical implications. By engaging with these resources, users can deepen their knowledge, hone their skills, and effectively utilize DeepSeek to its fullest potential.

A fundamental text to consider is "Artificial Intelligence: A Guide to Intelligent Systems" by Michael Negnevitsky. This book offers a broad introduction to AI concepts and methodologies, which serve as a solid groundwork for understanding how DeepSeek operates. Negnevitsky covers essential topics such as machine learning, neural networks, and data mining, all of which are integral to the functionality of DeepSeek. This resource is particularly beneficial for beginners looking to familiarize themselves with the core principles that underpin AI technologies.

For those seeking practical applications, "Hands-On Machine Learning with Scikit-Learn, Keras, and TensorFlow" by Aurélien Géron is highly recommended. This guide delves into machine learning techniques and provides step-by-step tutorials that can be directly applicable to DeepSeek. Géron's practical approach helps users learn how to implement AI solutions effectively, ensuring they can leverage DeepSeek's capabilities in real-world scenarios. The hands-on exercises included in the book encourage experimentation, fostering a deeper understanding of how to manipulate datasets and train models.

Another insightful resource is "Deep Learning" by Ian Goodfellow, Yoshua Bengio, and Aaron Courville. This book is considered a definitive text on deep learning, offering an in-depth exploration of the principles and practices that drive modern AI applications. It discusses advanced topics such as convolutional networks and recurrent networks, which are relevant to users looking to explore the more intricate functionalities of DeepSeek. By engaging with this text, users can gain a richer perspective on how deep learning techniques can be utilized to enhance their projects and research.

Lastly, "Data Science for Business" by Foster Provost and Tom Fawcett provides a strategic view of how data science intersects with business decision-making. This book emphasizes the importance of data-driven insights and analytics, which are crucial when effectively using DeepSeek to derive actionable conclusions. By understanding the business implications of AI and data analysis, users will be better equipped to implement DeepSeek in ways that align with organizational goals and drive success. Engaging with these recommended readings will undoubtedly empower users to unlock the full potential of DeepSeek and navigate the evolving landscape of artificial intelligence.

Training and Certification Options

Training and certification options play a crucial role in maximizing the potential of DeepSeek, an advanced AI tool designed to streamline data analysis and enhance decision-making processes. For users looking to master DeepSeek, understanding the various training programs available is essential. These programs cater to different skill levels, ensuring that both beginners and advanced users can benefit from structured learning paths that enhance their proficiency with the tool.

Many organizations offer official DeepSeek training courses, which can be accessed online or in person. These courses typically cover the fundamentals of DeepSeek, including installation, configuration, and basic functionalities. As users progress, they can delve into more complex topics such as advanced data querying techniques, machine learning integration, and real-time analytics. These structured courses not only provide theoretical knowledge but also include practical exercises that allow users to apply what they have learned in real-world scenarios.

In addition to official training courses, community-driven resources are invaluable for users seeking to deepen their understanding of DeepSeek. Online forums, user groups, and social media platforms host discussions where users can share tips, troubleshoot issues, and exchange ideas. Participating in these communities can enhance learning and provide support as users navigate the intricacies of the tool. Additionally, webinars and workshops led by experienced users often complement formal training, providing insights into best practices and innovative applications of DeepSeek.

Certification programs are another essential component of the training landscape. Upon completing specific training courses, users can pursue certification to validate their skills and knowledge of DeepSeek. Certifications not only boost a user's credibility but also demonstrate a commitment to professional development in the field of AI and data analysis. Many employers recognize these certifications, which can enhance job prospects and career advancement opportunities for users in various industries.

Finally, continuous learning is vital in the fast-evolving landscape of AI and data technologies. As DeepSeek updates its features and capabilities, users should actively seek out new training options and refresh their skills regularly. Subscribing to newsletters, following industry leaders on social media, and attending conferences can help users stay informed about the latest developments and training opportunities. By prioritizing ongoing education, users can ensure they are making the most of DeepSeek and remaining competitive in their respective fields.

Chapter 10: Conclusion

Recap of Key Lessons

In this subchapter, we will recap the key lessons learned throughout "DeepSeek Essentials: Unlocking AI Potential for Beginners." Understanding the fundamentals of DeepSeek is crucial for users aiming to master this powerful AI tool. This recap will highlight the essential concepts and practical applications that are critical for harnessing the full potential of DeepSeek in various contexts.

One of the primary lessons emphasized is the importance of data quality. Users have learned that the effectiveness of DeepSeek is directly proportional to the quality of the data fed into the system. High-quality, clean, and relevant data increases the likelihood of generating accurate insights and predictions. This lesson underscores the need for users to develop skills in data preparation and preprocessing, ensuring that the input data aligns with the intended outcomes of their AI projects.

Another significant takeaway from this book is the understanding of DeepSeek's core functionalities and features. Users have explored various capabilities, such as natural language processing, data visualization, and predictive analytics. Mastering these functionalities allows users to effectively manipulate and analyze data, leading to informed decision-making. Familiarity with these features is vital, as they equip users with the necessary tools to explore complex datasets and extract meaningful insights.

Collaboration and iterative learning have also emerged as key lessons in the journey of mastering DeepSeek. Engaging with a community of users provides opportunities for knowledge sharing and support. Users have been encouraged to leverage forums, workshops, and online resources to enhance their understanding and application of DeepSeek. This collaborative approach fosters continuous improvement and innovation, enabling users to stay updated with the latest developments in AI technology.

Lastly, ethical considerations in AI usage have been highlighted as an essential aspect of learning. Users are reminded of the responsibility that comes with deploying AI tools like DeepSeek. Understanding the implications of data privacy, bias, and transparency is crucial for ethical AI practice. By being aware of these considerations, users can ensure that their applications of

DeepSeek not only yield positive outcomes but also align with ethical standards and contribute to societal well-being. This lesson reinforces the need for a thoughtful and responsible approach to AI implementation.

The Importance of Embracing AI

Embracing artificial intelligence (AI) is crucial for users looking to harness the full potential of tools like DeepSeek. As technology continues to evolve at an unprecedented pace, incorporating AI into various processes can significantly enhance efficiency and productivity. Users who adapt to these advancements are not only better equipped to tackle complex challenges but also positioned to leverage AI's strengths in their daily tasks. By embracing AI, users can automate repetitive processes, gain insights from data, and ultimately make more informed decisions.

One of the primary benefits of adopting AI is its ability to analyze vast amounts of data quickly and accurately. In a world where information overload is a common challenge, AI tools like DeepSeek can filter through extensive datasets to identify patterns and trends that might otherwise go unnoticed. This capability enables users to streamline their operations and focus on strategic initiatives rather than being bogged down by mundane data handling. Thus, embracing AI allows users to transform raw data into actionable insights, driving better outcomes across various domains.

Furthermore, AI empowers users to personalize their experiences and offerings. Through machine learning algorithms, AI can learn from user interactions and preferences, tailoring recommendations and solutions to meet specific needs. For businesses, this means being able to provide customized services that enhance customer satisfaction and loyalty. Users who embrace AI can leverage these capabilities to create more engaging experiences and foster deeper connections with their audiences, ultimately leading to increased success in their endeavors.

In addition to improving efficiency and personalization, embracing AI fosters innovation and creativity. By automating routine tasks, users can allocate more time and resources to brainstorming and developing new ideas. AI can also be a catalyst for creativity, offering suggestions and alternatives that users may not have considered. In this way, AI not only enhances existing processes but also opens doors to new possibilities, allowing users to think outside the box and push the boundaries of their capabilities.

Finally, embracing AI is essential for remaining competitive in today's fast-paced environment. Organizations and individuals who resist adopting AI technologies risk falling behind their peers who are leveraging these tools for growth and success. The landscape of nearly every industry is rapidly changing due to AI advancements, making it imperative for users to stay informed and adaptable. By fully embracing AI and its potential, users can position themselves as leaders in their fields, ensuring they are not just participants in the future of work but active shapers of it.

Next Steps for DeepSeek Users

As DeepSeek users become more familiar with the platform, the next steps involve deepening their understanding and maximizing the tool's capabilities. The first step is to explore the comprehensive tutorials and documentation provided within the DeepSeek ecosystem. These resources offer detailed insights into various features, guiding users through the intricacies of the interface. Engaging with these tutorials not only enhances proficiency but also reveals hidden functionalities that can significantly improve productivity.

Once users have a solid grasp of the fundamental features, it is beneficial to participate in community forums and online discussions. Connecting with other DeepSeek users allows for the sharing of tips, troubleshooting techniques, and innovative use cases. These interactions foster a collaborative learning environment, where users can ask questions, share experiences, and learn from one another. Being part of such a community can also keep users updated on new developments and best practices, ensuring they remain at the forefront of AI utilization.

Another pivotal next step is to set specific goals for using DeepSeek. Whether it's improving data analysis, enhancing project management, or automating repetitive tasks, having clear objectives will help users focus their efforts. By identifying particular areas where DeepSeek can make a difference, users can tailor their learning and exploration to achieve meaningful results. This strategic approach not only enhances motivation but also leads to a more rewarding experience as users witness tangible improvements in their workflows.

In addition to goal setting, users should regularly assess their progress and adapt their strategies as needed. This can involve revisiting the tutorials or seeking out advanced resources that cater to evolving needs. An iterative approach to learning allows users to refine their skills continuously and stay agile in a rapidly changing technological landscape. By reflecting on their experiences and outcomes, users can better understand what works and make informed decisions about their next steps.

Finally, users should consider exploring integrations with other tools and platforms that complement DeepSeek. Many organizations utilize a suite of applications to streamline processes, and understanding how DeepSeek fits into this ecosystem can unlock even greater potential. By leveraging integrations, users can enhance data flow, improve collaboration, and create a more cohesive workflow. Taking these next steps will empower users to harness the full capabilities of DeepSeek, ultimately leading to enhanced efficiency and effectiveness in their projects.

www.ingramcontent.com/pod-product-compliance
Lightning Source LLC
LaVergne TN
LVHW052323060326
832902LV00023B/4574